AF584455

Claire Wheeler

Tara Clark

Can You SQUEEZE A Lemon?

For Alexander, Rowan and Oscar. My favourites. Love you forever
– Mum. (CW)

To the kids who are always busy, constantly creating and never stop chasing their dreams. You guys ROCK!
– Tara (TC)

First Published 2025 by
Redback Publishing
Suite 6, 13a Narabang Way,
Belrose NSW 2085
Australia

www.redbackpublishing.com
email: info@redbackpublishing.com

ISBN: 978-1-761401-31-2 – HBK

Author: Claire Wheeler
Illustrator: Tara Clark

A catalogue record for this book is available from the National Library of Australia

Claire Wheeler

Tara Clark

Can You SQUEEZE A Lemon?

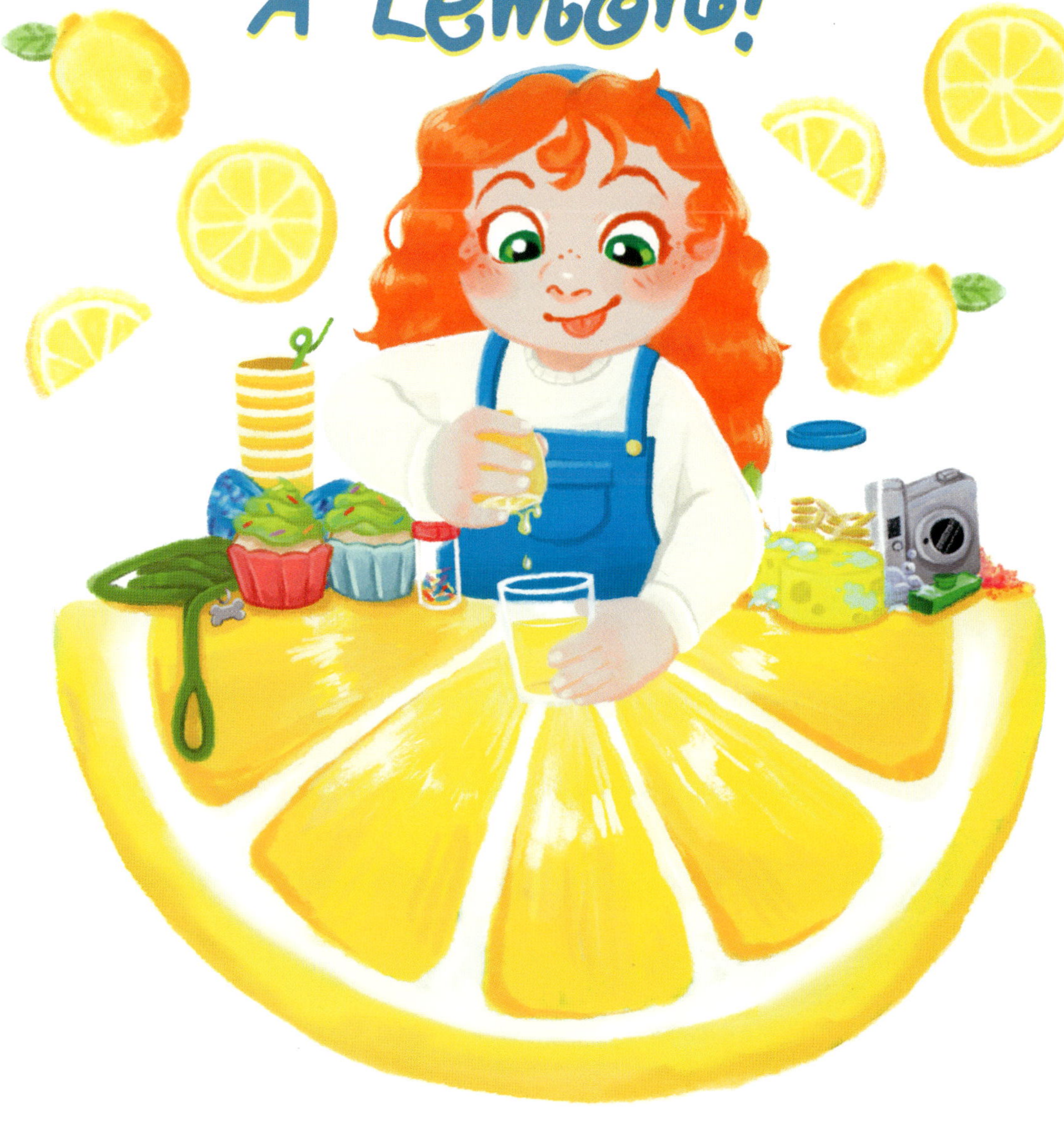

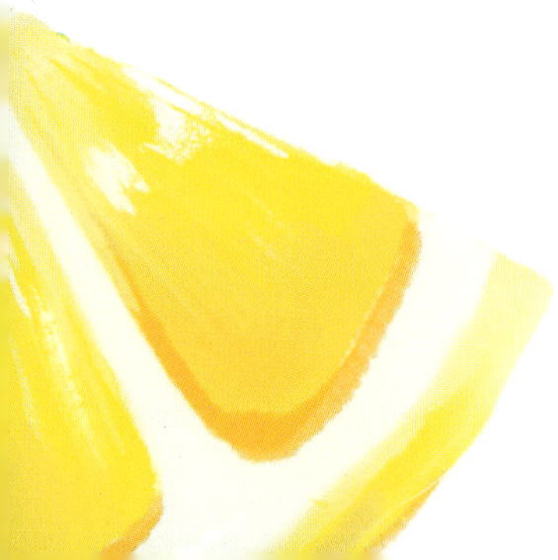

I have a lovely llama,
who dreams of **glitz** and **bling**,

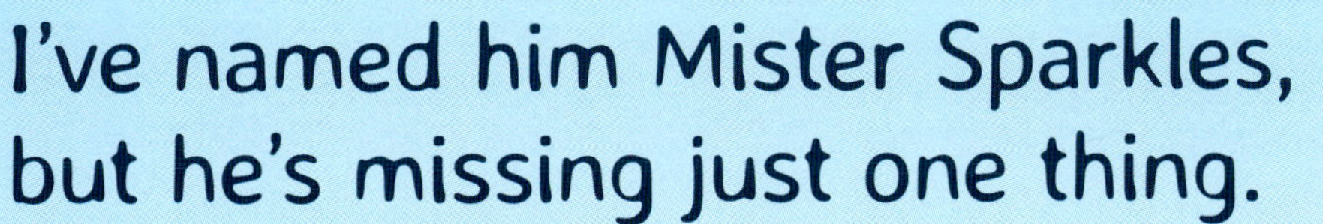

I've named him Mister Sparkles,
but he's missing just one thing.

Some sparkles are
what's missing,
to match his
shining name.

I need to save some money,
so that he can dress for fame.

My Mum suggested washing cars to earn some extra cash.

But then the hose
got tangled up and
gave our dog a splash.

Nan said, "Why not try walking dogs?
They'll follow you - you'll see!"

But dogs love racing
here and there,
which wasn't fun for me.

My neighbour said, "Start **busking**!
Play a tune, a catchy beat!"

But my kazoo was rusty,

and my music cleared the street.

My best friend, Sam, said,
"Cupcakes!

They could be a **tasty** treat!"

But what I made just
seemed to taste a bit like
Smelly feet.

My teacher shouted,

"**Photographs!**

Take pictures
we can keep!"

But the photos turned out fuzzy ...

things were looking
rather bleak.

Until Mum asked,
"Can you squeeze a lemon?"
She was grinning ear to ear.

I looked at her.

She looked at me.

We both let out a **cheer!**

I set out **squeezing** lemons,
a job I **loved** to do!

I made a stall with cups and all,
and soon there was a queue.

The kids lined up around the block
- they **loved** my lemonade!

I'd found a job that I could do,
and I was getting paid.

Soon I had a pile of cash
- much more than I had planned.

I took my llama shopping –

and **WOW**, did he look **grand!**

My llama is
now **famous**,
since he's taken
to the stage.

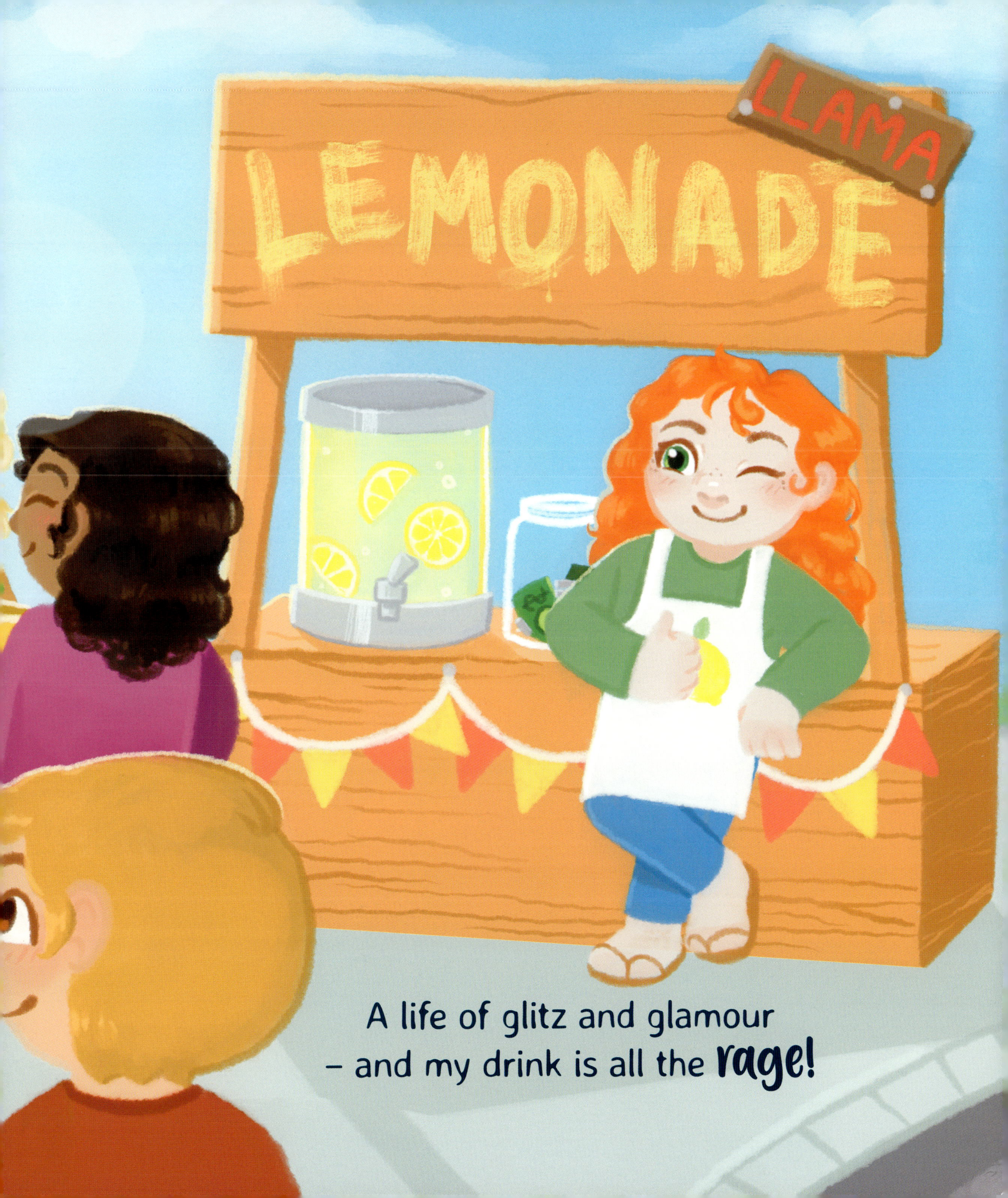

A life of glitz and glamour
– and my drink is all the **rage!**

I love my glitzy llama,
but he always wants more bling.
I'll have to
squeeze a lot
more lemons ...

If only he
could **sing**!!

HOW TO MAKE YOUR OWN LEMONADE!

GATHER YOUR ITEMS:

- 4 lemons
- 4 cups of water
- Ice
- Half a cup of sugar
- A large jug

STEP 1 Cut your lemons in half and squeeze the lemons to get all the lovely juice out.

(Make sure you ask a grown-up to help with this part.)

STEP 2 Remove all the seeds and pour the juice into your large jug.

STEP 3 Pour in your water and sugar. Remember to stir it well!

STEP 4 Taste your lemonade. If you think it's too sour, add a little bit more sugar. If it's too sweet, add a bit more water.

STEP 5 Add your ice to keep it extra cold. Then pour it into glasses for everyone to enjoy.

For extra fun, try adding half a cup of cranberry juice to make pink lemonade. Llama-licious!

About the author

Claire Wheeler has had a passion for entrepreneurship ever since she ran her own lemonade stand at the age of five. As the founder of Kid Biz Academy, a multi-award-winning Australian program for budding young entrepreneurs, Claire loves sparking big ideas in little minds, teaching kids how to follow their passions and turn their dreams into reality. When she's not busy hosting fun workshops and school events, Claire is writing stories at home in Newcastle with her husband and three lively boys, who all love hearing about her childhood business adventures. Claire hopes this book encourages you to try something new – who knows, you might even start your own lemonade stand (llama not included)!

About the illustrator

Tara Clark has been drawing since she could hold a crayon at two years old. Inspired by her love of reading, she illustrated her first book at just fifteen! An award-winning artist, Tara lives on the Central Coast with her family. While she doesn't own a llama, she does have seventeen cheeky chickens who also love a bit of glitz and bling. Even though they get into all sorts of trouble, the fluffy cuddles are worth it. Tara hopes her illustrations encourage young artists to embrace their creativity, no matter their style!